The Secrets of Positive Brainwashing

Stop Thinking In The 99 Percentile and Become The Financial 1%

Trainwashing

The Secrets of Positive Brain Washing

Michaelson Williams

Stop Thinking In The 99 Percentile and Become The Financial 1%

Copyright © 2012 Michaelson Williams

All rights reserved.

This book may not be reproduced, transmitted, or stored in whole or in part by any means, including graphic, electronic, or mechanical without the express written consent of the publisher except in the case of brief quotations embodied in critical articles and reviews.

Unless otherwise indicated, all intellectual properties and ideas are the sole property of Michaelson Williams. All images herein are the sole property, purchased or used by permission of Michaelson Williams, represented by: Houston Barnes Corporate Attorney at The Barnes Law Firm PLLC.

Visit our Web site at www.hwfnet.com

Printed in the United States of America

4143606

ISBN-13: 978-0615760261 (HWFnet, LLC.)

ISBN-10: 0615760260

Table of Contents

PREFACE 8

ABOUT THE AUTHOR 13

WHAT IS "TRAINWASHING"? 14

WHAT IS THE ULTIMATE QUESTION YOU NEED TO ASK YOURSELF ABOUT THE WAY YOU THINK AND LIVE TODAY? 16

THE QUESTION: 17

CHAPTER 1: TRAINWASHING 18

CHAPTER 2: BIG GLASS DOOR 28

Senses Box/Room Diagram 37

CHAPTER 3: BABY STEPS 42

CHAPTER 4: OPPORTUNITY 52

Mind / Time Management 58

CHAPTER 5: VISION 63

Vision Boarding 64

Appreciation 67

CHAPTER 6: MAKE DEALS 70

CHAPTER 7: LEARN SOMETHING NEW 77

CHAPTER 8: NOT ENOUGH 82

Ethos 83

Maturity of Mind 84

CHAPTER 9: BRAIN FOOD 88

CHAPTER 10: REACTION, ACTION, ATTRACTION 93

Reaction 93

Coaching / Coasting 97

Action 98

Attraction 101

CHAPTER 11: ATTITUDE 104

CHAPTER 12: SUCCESS POSITION 112

CHAPTER 13: FACES 117

CHAPTER 14: THINKING / EMOTION 124

CHAPTER 15: THE LIST 129

TRAINWASHING LEARNING TOOLS....................................... 136

Preface

Reading this book I would like you to understand the old cliché "you can do whatever you set your mind to" is absolutely true. Under the right circumstances we are able to achieve true greatness. Nothing is outside of our reach or greater than our own abilities.

If you truly believe things are possible they become possible. Sometimes, all we need is the chance to prove ourselves to ourselves and a lot of times we do not seize the opportunity to do so. I have seen people do some truly amazing things but it has only happened in certain situations. Sometimes the amazing things we do are forced upon us by the situations in which we are in at any given moment. Being an accidental hero in an emergency situation is an example in which one can be amazing.

I have seen people do amazing things by taking the opportunity to put themselves in a place from which they chose in order to see how well they would perform. I have also seen people do amazing things even though they've been in the same situation for years, yet one day they decided to change and become amazing. Every situation in life gives us an opportunity to do something extraordinary, a chance to take a chance on passing or failing.

One thing I have noticed is a large number of people who do great things have a tendency to not take credit for what they've done. If you learn one thing from reading this book- learn that you have the power to do things yourself, and as you utilize this power of mind do not be afraid to take credit for that which was amazing.

People need to realize the strength in which they have within. We spend so much of our time being brainwashed into thinking we are (not) good enough, we are (not) strong enough, and that someone else or something controls every aspect of our lives. We spend so much of our time being brainwashed into mediocrity it is almost impossible to feel the realization of our own power. We spend so much of our time inundated with things that slow our life journey for greatness to an absolute crawl. It is time to change this way of thinking.

It's time for our minds as a collective to become awake, to push ourselves further than we have ever been pushed but not in a negative manner; in a positive manner and direction. The time for emotional decision-making as the first resort must cease or made a last resort. Critical thinking in every aspect of our lives needs to be moved into the forefront of our minds or we are destined to repeat the historical scary, downtrodden, dissidence of our ancestors.

We all have a responsibility to do our part as a collective mindset to rise above the standard thinking of today. We play a part in the general makeup of our society whether we like it or not. Therefore the part that each and every one of us plays should be one of a positive and helpful nature. Almost every day I meet someone new who has this idea something is just not right in the world.

This is the beginning of a collective manifestation of the human mind to move into a realm where individuals look at things and analyze them with critical thought. Positive and sympathetic critical thought will allow each person in our society to listen and hear one another bringing the collective mindset together for the greater good.

These days I try to interact with people by simply asking questions which will allow them to engage in critical thinking. I, in turn, enjoy conversations when people allow me to exercise my critical thinking, and separate myself from emotional reaction. I hope with reading this book you join me in engaging others in critical conversation in which we can allow our own bias to be pushed aside. Join me in discovering the true secrets to understanding how the power of our minds is able to allow us to have anything we want including the ability to help others achieve what they want to achieve in life.

By reading this book I anticipate you will be able to realize and understand control comes in many forms. Sometimes we try to control other people; sometimes others try to control us. Realize the most important control that can ever happen in life is the control you have over yourself. So the next time you sit down to watch television, which is only designed as a cog in your wheel of success, realize this is a form of control.

The next time you sit down in front of your computer and another new social media site tries to grab personal information from you to keep you in your same mundane life, move away. Realize this is a form of control. Once you realize these things are happening to keep you from reaching the pinnacle of your success I hope you comprehend you have the control to move away from these things.

Move away from the control and breathe the fresh air of self-control to gain financial greatness and success in life. Financial success is right at your fingertips. You are grabbing a hold of it right now because you are looking at this book. Be sure to use this book over and over as a tool to train and retrain success in your life. Become a deliberate hero to yourself, to your family, to your friends, to a stranger and do this for the rest of your life.

About The Author

Michaelson William, an entrepreneur, author, and critical thinker, applies a unique philosophy and psychology when thinking about success. Having been the CEO of multiple companies, involved in martial arts since the age of 4 ½ years old, a health and fitness consultant, and an avid student of psychology study, he developed a unique technique called "Trainwashing". He hopes his new Trainwashing techniques will assist others to be successful.

Michaelson possesses various degrees and professional certificates from business, martial arts, personal training, and security contracting. This gives Michaelson a broad perspective on how people and the human mind react to pressure when dealing with success and failure. Michaelson continues to educate himself in the ways of human thinking and behaviors in order to help others on a successful journey in life. Michaelson has already written several books in different genres but all are based on the functionality and psychology of the human mind.

What is "Trainwashing"?

From the time the first words were ever spoken to us the conditioning process and control mechanisms of "proper" behavior have been ingrained into our minds. All of our lives this conditioning or brainwashing has dictated every facet of how we live by telling us what to do in every waking moment, and even when we sleep. This brainwashing has controlled the level of success that one can attain in life and very few are able to break this extremely well embedded training.

Trainwashing is the act of washing the brain clean of the lifelong brainwashing of family, friends, religious leaders, media, big business advertising, and government which keep us thinking like the "have-nots" in the 99 percentile. Through proper training the brain is washed clean of this lifelong negative conditioning and in its place retrained or "Trainwashed" with 100% positive brainwashing.

The secrets of training the brain through repeated Trainwashing, to accept new positive brainwashing and conditioning of mind, are to be found within the pages of this book. Once the freed mind is on a course of action to think Trainwashing has begun to take place.

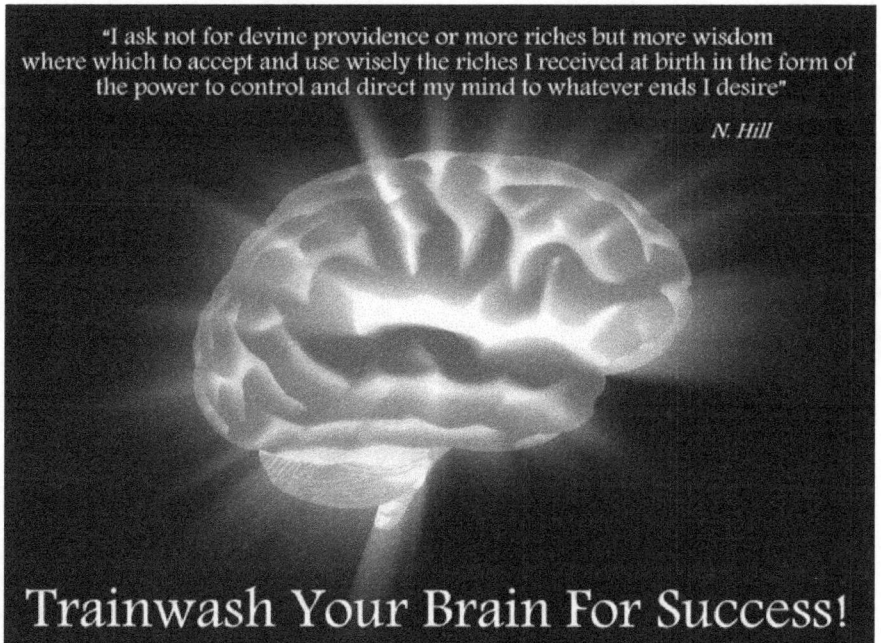

What is the ultimate question you need to ask yourself about the way you think and live today?

Before you are able to fully understand what "Trainwashing" is you must first ask yourself the ultimate question about why you think the way you think today. Once this question has been fully accepted and understood only then shall you be able to "Trainwash" your brain in order to achieve complete success.

The Question:

Ask yourself with complete honesty why do you believe what you believe today, right now in life?

The answer to this question is you believe what you believe and think the way you think because you have been conditioned or brainwashed to do so. Nothing more. When you are ready to accept this fact only then will the contents of this book be helpful enough for you to make the necessary changes in life to achieve great success. Let go of the bonds which have rendered you stagnant and get ready to move forward and upward as you learn the secrets of "Trainwashing".

Chapter 1: Trainwashing

Brain Training

Being successful in a world where most people believe success can only be for the few can be a daunting task. Our minds are not trained to be successful on a grand scale. We are conditioned to think and believe otherwise until life has passed us by. Then we feel it is too late for true success. Most people do believe they can make small successes in life but at the same time believe the greater successes in life are unattainable. True success is for the "other guy", is what people tell themselves. People feel guilty about creating success for themselves.

I will go one step further to say people feel guilty about the mere thought of being successful or deserving success. We think of every excuse we can come up with as to why we shouldn't achieve success in life. We point the finger at others to blame them for our lack of success. We dream of success but only as something which is wishful thinking but not truly attainable. So how do we change this way of thinking?

I came up with the new psychological idea and term "Trainwashing" because it is the act of reversing a lifetime of negative brainwashing. Our entire lives we have been trained in a manner that keeps us unsuccessful. Every aspect of our life is monitored and guided to keep our success or lack thereof at a certain level. We are told in some way shape or form when to eat, when to sleep, when to work, when to rest, when to recreate, when to procreate and at the best we barely recognize this is going on.

Most people will go through their entire life without recognizing they are even being brainwashed. In order to figure out you are being brainwashed into living and acting a certain way you have to possess the ability to step outside of yourself. We all have the ability to step away from our trapped way of life in order to look in at ourselves from the outside. The problem is we are too consumed with "busy work" and things that have little meaning in the grand scheme of life. The more inundated you are with "busy work" the less likely you are to actually recognizing the brainwashing systems in place in your life right now.

Trainwashing is retraining your mind through **self positive brainwashing**. A great deal of our negative brainwashing is self inflicted, and most of the brainwashing has taken place since childhood. Brainwashing may seem extremely negative as you think about it because of the negative connotation surrounding the word brainwashing.

Stop Thinking In The 99 Percentile and Become The Financial 1%

When we think of the word brainwashing we think of it in only a negative fashion. When we think of brainwashing we think of someone taking control of our minds in order to make us do or feel a certain way that is usually surrounded by negativity. For the most part this is true.

What I'm saying is turn the negative brainwashing into positive brainwashing by retraining your mind in a positive manner. If we know we have been brainwashed since early childhood and brainwashing dictates every aspect of our life then we understand how the process works. We understand we live our lives a certain way right now. If we can recognize this life we live right now, and we really do not understand how we got this way, then there must be a control factor in place. We know we have arrived at this place, at this juncture in our life through a process in which we believe is natural.

If you believe the house you purchased, the job you have, the car you drive, the food you eat, and your health, is a product of your decision-making alone you are absolutely wrong. Everything I have mentioned has been manipulated in your everyday life. If you are unwilling to look at these things and accept you are brainwashed you will not be able to undo what has been done to you. It would be very simple for me to just state that everyone has the power of freewill to determine their path to future success. But how can a person have complete freewill if every aspect of their life has been slowly and methodically manipulated in order for someone else to make billions of dollars?

If you are the person who is willing to investigate and understand you have been brainwashed then change and success is just around the corner. If you are this person then the "Trainwashing" can begin. You can start to reroute the circuitry which has kept you unsuccessful and begin to retrain your mind into a manner that will make you truly successful.

Negative brainwashing is no more powerful than positive brainwashing. Brainwashing is brainwashing so it carries the same weight in our lives. The only difference is the time that has elapsed in which a person has been negatively brainwashed. If you want to understand a major product of negative brainwashing, just monitor the number of hours in which you watch television each week. Then look at the purchased products in your home and life which have been influenced by what you have seen on television.

If you are in your early 20s and you want to realize how brainwashed a person is, speak to a family member who's in their late 30s or early 40s. Sometimes you do not even have to speak to them. You can just observe them, look at the way they're living, what they're driving, where they work, what they eat, look at what they choose for entertainment, and the level of negative brainwashing will reveal itself.

If you decide to take the observation a step further and actually question the family member or friend you choice to observe, find out how their life path was chosen. Your subject is likely oblivious to why they are at the place in life they're at currently. People who are negatively brainwashed are not likely to remember the decisions they made which lead them to an unsuccessful outcome in life.

People who are negatively brainwashed are more likely to see their lives as a blur. People may remember a wrong turn here or there in life but are not going to remember every move that led them to less than what they expected from life. The person who never gives up on their dreams is not likely to treat these wrong turns as negative. Instead this person's view has changed and the "wrong turns" are now viewed as positive lessons and periods of necessary growth.

The wonderful thing about positive brainwashing or "Trainwashing" is there is no time in your life in which it will not work. You can retrain your brainwashing at in any point of your life. There is nothing which can stop you other than yourself when it comes to retraining your brainwashing. Success is in the control of every person on this planet. Retraining the mind for success is within the grasp of anyone who is willing to accept they have been negatively brainwashed into a certain lifestyle.

Sometimes we experience guilt about success and this will halt their ability to move forward. Training your mind to respond to success without guilt is simple. When the slightest bit of success enters your life and the feeling of guilt or "I don't deserve this" creeps in, simply retrain that thought. It's not good enough to retrain the thought just at the moment in which it enters the mind. This is where you train yourself to brainwash yourself or use the Trainwashing methods. There is extra work which has to go into retraining your brainwashing from negative to positive.

When the guilt of success set in and you've told yourself "I don't deserve this" it is then that you have to start the positive brainwashing. This is the point where you sit down take a pen and piece of paper and write down why you deserve this bit of success you have just achieved and received. This exercise of "Trainwashing" has to be done over and over and over again.

Think about when you're trying to remember someone's phone number (although with the technology of smart phones we barely have to commit anything to memory these days). Nevertheless think about something you had to remember, you had to commit to your long-term memory and think about how you complete the task. When we are trying to remember things in our long-term memory we write things down repeatedly, we rehearse them, we visualize until it becomes remembered. This is a form of brainwashing. Although this is not behavioral remembering it is still away to training something new into the brain.

Using the same techniques, and principles we can eliminate guilty feelings of not deserving our little successes in life. Once we start to eliminate the guilt then we can appreciate our successes and from there more success will come. Responding positively to successes which are achieved in life will allow you to make decisions that are more positive.

Open minded good decisions without fear or guilt for becoming successful will help you to achieve greater success. Training yourself to be open minded and to look at things without blinders on will allow you to be able to see success as it's coming into your life. In the beginning it is very difficult to "Trainwash" your mind. You must be unrelenting in the

"Trainwashing" exercises in order to keep the positive flow of ideas and positive energy coming in.

There will be times when you will achieve certain goals and the enjoyment will be there in the beginning then all of a sudden the guilt comes in. This is a normal part of the process and should not be viewed in a negative way. Things that are worthwhile take hard work. Take no shortcuts and persevere. When the guilt or negativity tries to creep into your life just stop, reset, and train something positive in its place. Appreciate what you have done and what you have achieved. Give yourself approval, and then say to yourself and repeat, "I deserve the success I just achieved".

Re-brainwash success into your mind. Think about your "Trainwashing" techniques as if it were a light bulb. When you first put in the light bulb it shines brilliantly. It illuminates the entire room. Over time this illumination becomes dull and your light starts to flicker as it's getting ready to burn out. Before the bulb actually burns out replace the bulb with a new bulb. This means the ideas you used to train positive brainwashing have to be rejuvenated.

It is normal to take a few steps back in the process of gearing your mind to accept success. The most important part is to be able to recognize, understand, and then stop the negative process. Sometimes in the process of Trainwashing our mind we get inundated with life and we aren't able to see we are slipping, or losing hold of our successes.

Sometimes we fall back into our same routine because the negative brainwashing has been there for so long. This is where we have to train ourselves to recognize these small slips and falls are part of the process, they can be changed, and then we move forward again.

The Secrets of Positive Brainwashing

Your brain is like a box where you store information; there is no magic in this box. You can only pull out what you put into the box" Michaelson Williams

Chapter 2: Big Glass Door

The Box or Room with the Sixth Sense

Let's think about Trainwashing in another way. The successes and failures we've had to date, as well as the successes and failures we can imagine for the future, all stem from our life experiences since childhood. From early childhood we use our five senses in order to judge and guide us through this experience we call our life. We rely on what we see, our sense of sight. We rely on our sense of smell.

Our sense of touch sends signals to our brain about what is hot, cold, or has texture. We absorb this information for later use in life. We rely on our sense of hearing to get messages from other people who tell us how we are to live this life experience. Our sense of taste allows us to eat certain things, which bring us pleasure or make us gag. These are the five senses we are very aware of them because we use them daily.

So we know that our five senses are activated from birth in order to create this experience that we call life. Our five senses guide us on our journey of life until we are old and gray and our senses begin to fail. The human senses allow us to have perceptions of what is good, bad, what we are doing right, and what we are doing wrong during our life experiences.

But these five senses are not always accurate in developing the experiences that will allow for a completely successful life. Furthermore, they may not allow humans to be able to attract and manifest whatever it is that we want in life. These five senses can be tricked into giving false feedback which will completely hinder whether we are able to attract into our lives a life that is completely successful.

In our human experience we also have a sixth sense. The sixth sense is very much a part of our entire life's experience and may be the most important sense that we have and yet the least utilized. I would go even further to say that our sixth sense is the one that we trust the least but is the most important to develop in order to achieve and attract into our life everything that we wish.

First let's talk about the five senses and how they apply to the human experience and how it applies to what you can attract into your life or into this experience. Then I will discuss how the very important senses apply to the Trainwashing experience.

Think about everything you experience in life from childhood as if it is a box or room in which information is stored. I say a box or room because our minds are mass storage centers which store and keep all of the data in our lives. The information that you take in to this box or this one room is the information that you will be able to pull from at a later date whether conscious or unconscious.

In the end, this box or room contains your complete life experience and is also the fabric of how you live and think about the value and quality of your life. The information that you put into this box or that is put into this room by others is the information that you are able to pull out to utilize during this life experience. Now obviously we do not choose all of the information that we put into our boxes or our room on our own.

The information that goes into this room when we are children is mostly dictated by our parents or guardian. This information, believe it or not, is the beginning of your brainwashing. Yes, Brainwashing. The information that is put into our mind, into this room, can be positive brainwashing or negative brainwashing. So how does this box or room work for and against us as we strive for better life and human experience? Let's say within the contents of this box or room we have at the top one big window.

We also have within this space five separate doors, the last one being a **Big Glass Door**. We were born with this window and five doors. The window and doors are your five senses and one sense you are less aware at this point in life, your sixth sense. The window at the top is your sight. The first door below the window is your sense of smell. The second door is your sense of touch. The third door is hearing. The fourth is taste. The filth big glass door is your sixth sense.

Now these five doors and one window are our entire life experience. Everything that happens to you, everything you learn, everything that you do, and how you live, are contained within this space. So let's touch on each of the components of this space from a different point of view. Starting with the four doors in which you have almost complete trust. The first door, smell, you absolutely trust that what you smell is exactly what it should be. Next, you trust in what you touch. Therefore whatever you touch, its texture, whether smooth or rough, you trust that what you're touching is believable.

Third, your hearing, which you trust based on the sounds that go into your ears, register in your brain exactly what it should be. You do not mistake a car horn for a train horn or a baby crying for an airplane flying overhead. The next door that you trust is taste. You know if something tastes good to you and you know if something tastes bad to you. If something tastes good then you savor and enjoy the taste. There are also direct signals to the brain which increase the amount of enjoyment. On the other hand, if something tastes bad to you, you may spit it out.

The next item in this box or room is your window or your sight. This window is at the top of your other four major senses and the less aware sixth sense. You trust what you see because sight is one of the most important senses that we have to create (in a normal situation) life experiences. If we think about it, sight is probably the most important sense that we think we have in our awareness of emotional experiences.

You think that what you see is true and to your brain this is correct. For the most part the sight window, as it applies to our room, is a very reliable sense with the exception of when it comes to negative brainwashing. When it comes to negative brainwashing your sight will betray you every single time. The reason your eye sight can betray you is because your sight cannot pick up if someone is trying to deliberately deceive you.

This applies to humans in non face to face interaction and as it relates to our sight space in our room or box.

The sense that we rely on the most, sight, is one that can be deceived or used against us negatively in order to alter our life's experience. You may be saying "well I trust what I see more than anything" but have you ever attended a magic show and tried to figure out exactly what the magician had done in order to trick you into thinking he sawed a woman in half? No matter how hard you look at the trick your eyes and brain could not figure out exactly how it was done.

From your experience the woman was sawed in half. Your brain believed even though logic and reason tell you it did not happen. In your mind you still believe the woman was cut completely in half right before your eyes. So here's my point, the more you program through visual stimulation, negativity and lack of success ,or things that do not bring you success and will not bring you success, the less likely you are to become successful.

What you put into the box or into your room which became your life experience is what you will get out. There is no other way. You cannot pull information from this space that you have not put into the box, that is unless you learn to access the Big Glass Door. Everything that you believe in life right now to this day was either forcibly or voluntarily made a part of your experience. Therefore the clean and clear window that you received at birth is now smudged and dirtied with the negative experiences of your life.

These smudges that are put on this flawless piece of glass which bring you joy every time you look through it are placed there by your parents, friends, as well as what you watch on television, listen to on your headphones, and what is deliberately programmed into your mind on a daily bases.

The very first time you ever heard the word "no" that was a smudge on your window. The background noise that you hear without noticing through media programming is additional smudges on your window. After some time your window gets so cloudy that you can no longer see through it, it no longer brings pleasure into your experience.

The clarity and focus that was once seen through this window is now dusty, cloudy, and full of fingerprints and smudges from other people that you have interacted with during this experience. Every once in a while we take a paper towel and some cleaner and we clean up a portion of our window. We can see clearly through it for a short period of time until we let someone smudge our window once again.

How does all of this apply to the psychology of Trainwashing? In simple terms, you must clean your window as often as possible. Once your window is clean the information that you see, hear, or experience which smudges the window must interrupt your good experiences in life. The act of Trainwashing is constantly cleaning your window, constantly not allowing other people to smudge or dirty this window which is the mind. Trainwashing is about not allowing you to smudge your own window by the music that you pump into your head which is negative. The hours and hours of television watching not only completely cloud the window but taints the entire space of the box or room that is your mind.

From the time of your birth and even now you have in your possession a sixth sense. This sixth sense is your **Big Glass Door.** When you are first born to this Earth and into the body that you possess right now your big glass door was open. Now the sixth sense and the big glass door is the most important door that you can have in your room or in the mind space. The reason the big glass door is most important is because this is the door which allows you to attract positive things into your experiences and into your life.

The big glass door that is within this room is, or was previously, opened to fantasy and imagination. The big glass door allows you to manifest whatever you desire into your experience. The big glass door allowed you to sit down with your dolls as a child and create an entire life and experience that was wonderful and dreamy.

The big glass door, or the sixth sense, allowed you to pick up a stick to fight the biggest dragons and to be the best swordsman in all of the land. Until someone told you that he or she did not exist the big glass door housed an imaginary friend who shared your adventures. More importantly the big glass door allowed you to think about a toy or a vacation to Disney when you were a child and allowed you to create and make those things come into your life.

The Secrets of Positive Brainwashing

Senses Box/Room Diagram

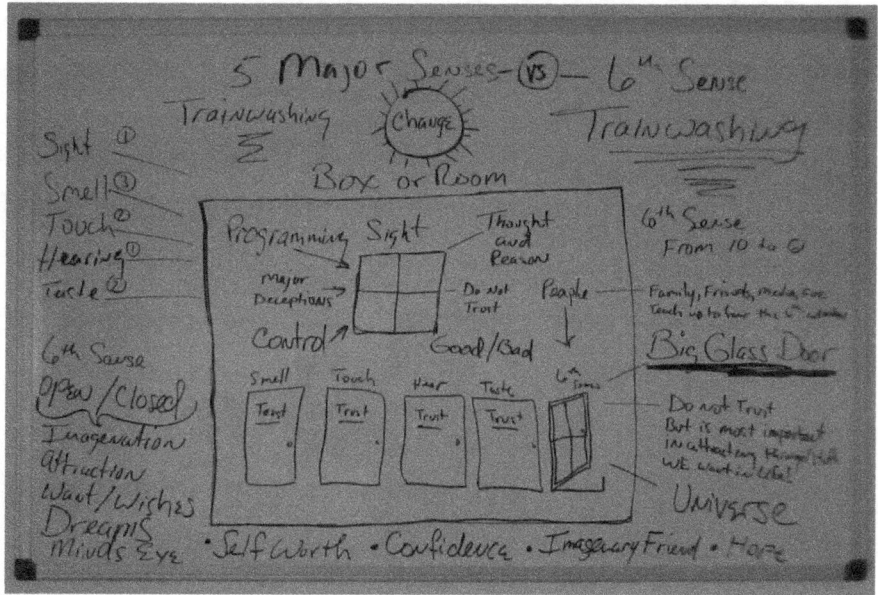

Today we trust in our window with all the smudges, but yesterday when we were children we trusted in our big glass door. From the time you were a child until now you've been taught by your parents and by what you watch on television, or listen to in music, to close your big glass door. Negative brainwashing caused you to close your big glass door and for most of us we not only lock the door but we have completely erased the big glass door from our experience.

Now that you are "an adult" you no longer use anything in the box or room other than your smudged window and the other four remaining doors. The big glass door is still there for some of us but you have been taught to fear not only thinking about the door, but to ever, ever use the door again.

The wonderful thing about this box or room that is our life experience is we can always change what's going on inside of this space. Therefore, if you use the principles of Trainwashing to clean your window you can then see clear enough to recreate the big glass door. Once you recreate the big glass door in your room, and have a clean window along with the other four doors, you can open the big glass door.

Once you open that big glass door again you can manifest all of the things that you were able to manifest and attract into your experience when you were a child. When you were a child you really had no understanding of this box or this room and yet you were able to bring things into your life effortlessly.

Once you became "an adult" and you had absorbed enough of the negative brainwashing, you lost the power to utilize and even see the big glass door. I would suggest that the only time we should look into our past is to once again find our big glass door. Look into your own past, find your big glass door, and open it.

Once you open your big glass door bring into it the things that you wish to have including: happiness, health, wealth, true friends, loving family, and whatever else you choose and envision in your life experience. Find your sixth sense and use it as it is supposed to be used, and that is to bring you happiness in this life.

You may be thinking how do I get my sixth sense back? How do I get my fifth door back into my box, back into my room, and back into my experience? **Simply Meditate.** If you sit or lie down on the floor and meditate you will be able to clean your window in order for the big glass door to reappear. The longer you meditate the better. This does not mean to sit or lay on the floor and meditate for three hours. Rather, over the next few weeks and months that you meditate you will have fully and completely learned to control everything that happens in this space.

You will have learned to control the doors and the window in this room. When you are comfortable in this space there will be absolutely nothing that you cannot accomplish in this life. You will be able to open the big glass door and pull into your life exactly what you want, new car, new relationships, new house, huge bank accounts, and anything else you desire.

Once you bring the big glass door back into your room, in order to keep the big glass door, you must keep your window clean. If you allow smudges on your window the big glass door will close once again and disappear from your room. Teach yourself to Trainwash your mind so that you can once again clean your window.

Manifest your big glass door, which again is your sixth sense, and then be able to use that door to create a better and wonderful life for yourself. All of the things that caused your window to become smudged keep them out of your box and out of your experience. If you can control everything that happens within this box or your room then you can control everything that happens in your life and experience while in this life.

The Secrets of Positive Brainwashing

"The storm is here and now. The rains come and water floods our lives. Nothing last forever and the rainbow always appears"

Michaelson Williams

Chapter 3: Baby Steps

Creating a New You through Baby Steps

Everything in life is a process. We did not get to the point where we are without this process. If we are unsuccessful right now there was a process that took place. If we are semi-successful in our life it was a process that took place. If we are considered or consider ourselves super successful there still was a process that took place. We do not get from point A to point B without a process taking place which reveals the end result (Success or Failure).

The wonderful thing about this process is at any point during this journey the process or processes can change. Most of us think becoming successful is a huge leap forward. The reason we think this way is because we look at where we are now and we look at what we perceive as successful, not in a linear fashion, but as some quantum leap.

We look at the beginning of the journey and we look at the end but leave out the middle. It is the middle of the journey that is most important. The reason I say the middle of the journey is most important is because in the beginning of the journey is the quitting phase. At the end of the journey is the success phase. The middle of the journey is the true work phase of the process.

Let's talk about the quitting phase or the beginning of the journey. When people make a decision to do something they are extremely fired up about the decision. People start the work, they are excited, energized, and raring to go. And then the work begins. When people figure out it's going to take a great deal of work to become successful they question whether it's worth it, if they're worth it.

At this milestone the notion to quit or create excuses becomes easier than moving forward toward the goal. During this quitting phase is when the negative brainwashing carries an extreme amount of weight. This is where most people decide to quit or to stop their journey.

On the other hand the success phase is realized because we have the things we want. The success phase exists because we can do the things we want to do in life. If you are in the success phase of your journey you are living in the moment. During this success phase you can barely realize what the middle of the journey was although you will remember the beginning.

You will remember at the beginning of the journey you were poor, you did not know where your next meal was coming from, you remember your car was insufficient, you remember your clothes were worn, your bank account was small etc. Because everyone goes through different phases on the journey to success, we remember in phases. Some parts we leave out on purpose and for whatever reason other parts mean much more to us. The length of time that we spend on our journey to success will determine how much each phase of the journey we remember and how we remember each event.

Successful people who are living in the moment of success usually have to sit down and recap the processes which took them through the middle of the journey. The reason the middle of the journey less important while in the success phase is because this phase is in the past. There is very little need to think about the past when you're in the success phase of your journey, because you are having so much fun in the success phase.

So how do you get from this quitting phase to the success phase of the journey? The answer or key to this question is through the middle phase. There has to be smaller steps taken or "Baby Steps". It is the middle of the journey in which the baby steps are applied and are most important.

Without the middle of the journey there can be no success phase even though in the success phase of the journey we hardly ever think about the past.

In the beginning of the journey or the quitting phase we have to quickly apply baby steps to the "Trainwashing" process. Without delay, from the time you make a decision to take the steps in order to be successful in life and on your journey to retrain your brain for success, baby steps have to be implemented. Without this process of retraining the mind through smaller chunks, failure becomes more prominent.

Utilizing baby steps to retrain your mind for success can be applied by setting goals which are so small you can barely recognize any positive brainwashing at all. Here are a few examples: take your favorite television show you feel you just cannot live without and analyze the television show. Actually sit down with the notepad and analyze the television show to find out what content in this show will help you to become a success.

Start out by listing 10 things within the time span of the television show, including commercials, which are aiding in your journey to success. If after watching this television show and the commercials you do not have a list of 10 things which helps you to personally become successful, eliminate this show. Take the baby step to eliminate television shows from your life and then replace it with something of equal value to you which will assist you in the process of becoming more successful.

Taking baby steps to eliminate television shows opens up wasted time which is slowing down the process of you becoming successful. Here is another example: let's take a technology addiction such as using a cell phone or text messaging. So many people spend huge amounts of time texting etc which can be used for "Trainwashing" your brain for success.

We have been brainwashed into thinking that without technology or without our cell phone and our text messaging we cannot do anything. Believe it or not these things are in no way needed for most people and will slow down the success process. Even if you do need technology to become successful people still rely on technology too much.

So if you find yourself text messaging or using social media for the majority of your day, you are impeding the success process. Your journey for success is being slowed by unnecessary activity. Therefore you must take baby steps in order to slow this addiction and replace it with something that breeds success.

The third richest man in the world, Warren Buffett, is believed to not own a cell phone or use social media in his success journey. He surely has people in place to take care of daily business activity and those people have cell phones etc.

Here is the question: what makes you more important than the third richest person on the planet at this time? If the third richest man in the world can become this way without the use of social media or cell phones then you should ask yourself how much you should be using these vices.

Once you discover that these technologies are mostly noise which slows down your journey for success only then can you take the necessary baby steps to eliminate some of its use. Some of you are thinking right at this moment I cannot live without my cell phone. I cannot live without (FB) or some other social media or technology. IF this is the case and you cannot take baby steps to change this idea, then success will be further down the road than you can ever imagine.

Taking baby steps to retrain the mind means taking steps to change you. The new you will be able to manage these baby steps through the middle of the journey. The new you will be taking the baby steps to "Trainwash" your mind into thinking and believing things which seem important now are not truly important for the achievement of success. Take a different path so that you can achieve a different result in life. Eliminate the noises of mediocrity.

Once you have lived without these technology crutches, which seem extremely important right now for a period of time, you can recognize how unimportant they really are. You are brainwashed into thinking you need this technology so someone else can become successful off of your brainwashed habits.

When you are inundated with these things you are helping to create success and wealth for someone else, not you. Once you recognize and can control the things which are not making you successful you are able to fill your life with things that will make you successful.

During the baby step process it is very important to recognize and implement both self-motivation and empowerment of self. Every step of the way in the journey, and especially in the middle of the journey, you must brainwash yourself into a mind that is able to self motivate. There must be a sense of empowerment of self which allows you to be better than the day before.

Self-motivation and true empowerment is not very difficult to accomplish if you apply baby steps to the process. All it takes is small processes and implementation of tools which will show you how to be self-important. You do not have to sit down and read an entire book on how to self-motivate or how to become empowered.

Because this is a journey or a process, simply reading a paragraph every night will cause positive change. Believe it or not your initial brainwashing took time through very small steps and processes which could not be recognized by your brain. Therefore "Trainwashing" is achieved through the same slow processes, only in reverse.

Again, when we look at the journey in which we have become successful, sometimes we refused to look at it in very small minute chunks. This is much like how we would view reading a self-help book to promote self-motivation and empowerment. We look at the entire book and we say: "it's too long", "it's too much to read", or "I'm not a great reader". We come up with excuses of why we cannot finish the book when we haven't even started the book.

So the journey of educating yourself through self-help books should be small. Read a page or a half a paragraph each night and make it habitual. Take baby steps to deny negativity and then allow positive empowerment into your life to achieve success.

If reading isn't your cup of tea, get on the Internet and view videos about self-motivation and empowerment. Some people learn and understand better through visual-aids while others prefer reading. It does not matter how you get the information. All that matters is that it becomes ritualistic in your journey to success.

The Secrets of Positive Brainwashing

"Success is not final, failure is not fatal: it is the courage to continue that counts."

Winston Churchill

Chapter 4: Opportunity

Being There In the Mind Once the Doors Open

What does it mean to be there in "the mind" when the doors of opportunity are opening? Sometimes in our journey for success we are so focused on the journey in our minds we miss opportunities which are right in front of us. It is important that the mental receivers in your mind are open so you can catch the opportunities for success, no matter how large or small.

Some doors of opportunity are big and easy to see, easy to become excited about. Other doors of opportunity are small and harder to spot right away. Excitement cannot be generated about an opportunity you missed so be ready. Keep your mind set and trained to see the small openings as well as the large openings of opportunity for success. This idea is very important because sometimes the small doors or the small opportunities become the largest avenue for success.

Keep the mind ready, keep the mind focused, stay aware and alert. Make sure you do not approach any opportunity with a negative attitude. The next big idea may be one that seems to have little promise. This does not mean every opportunity is going to be the one which makes you successful but you can be assured a missed opportunity is one you will not become successful from.

Sometimes opportunities which create success in your life will need a little more nurturing than others. Make sure your mind is prepared to analyze an opportunity which comes your way and do so without fear of achieving success from the opportunity. Make sure if you are working on multiple opportunities at one time each are given the same amount of care and review until the best opportunity reveals itself.

A lot of times opportunities come from things we create ourselves. So keeping opportunities "at the ready" could mean you are always in a creative state of mind. If you are this type of person already it is going to be imperative that your mind stays in a creative mood. If you can keep the mind in a creative mode then others will be able to see and understand and then latch on to your ideas and opportunity.

This can come in the form of investors, supporters, someone taking interest in your project and willing to share with others through media sources. Keeping your creative mind on track can open up numerous opportunities for success. On the other hand, if you do not keep your mind "at the ready" by constantly being creative, then other people will not be able to see opportunity with you.

Some very simple ways to keep your mind in a creative state of being is to write, draw, or work with your hands, such as building something with wood or making clay sculptures. Do anything that will keep your mind active in a manner which inspires you mentally and emotionally. Be sure to be extremely positive in your choices of creative outlets.

Once the mindset has changed, in order to start taking steps to move towards success and a more successful life, there are changes which take place. Some of the changes are more obvious than others. There are subtle changes and then there are changes that are more recognizable in behavior, mannerisms, attitude etc. During this time there are also relapses where we take a few steps backward. When there are relapses they should be recognized and dealt with, and then move forward.

You may be asking yourself, how do I recognize a relapse in my own behavior that may set me back a few steps in my journey to success? When the setbacks come you will know it almost immediately because you will go from a positive attitude to a negative one or from happy to depressed.

Sometimes the setback comes from someone trying to steal your dream by telling you that you cannot do what you set out to do. Again recognize and deal with these incidental events and then move forward.

There are also times during this success growth and during the journey where ideas may come in abundance. This is what I call idea-overflow. Make sure your mind is ready for this overflows of ideas phase. This is when the mind is in such a highly creative state ideas flow abundantly and in odd times of the day or night. Basically, this is when the faucet of ideas is pouring out and these ideas will need to be managed. Not only will these ideas need to be managed they will also need to be catalogued and noted so there is nothing missed or forgotten.

In order to be prepared for this "idea overflow" you must have tools which will allow you to catalogue these ideas. The best thing you can do is to have notepads around your home so when these idea flashes hit you are able to write them down immediately.

There may be times when you wake up from a sound sleep and a dream resonates in your mind so vividly you are unable to return to sleep. You may not understand the dream at the moment but it is very important you write the dream as vividly and accurately as possible onto a notepad. There may be other times you are driving in your car and an idea comes to you. It is a good idea to purchase an app for your phone that will allow you to dictate notes on your phone.

This is a time when technology can serve you in a positive manner. There is a big difference between letting technology work for you and being a slave to technology. Dictating notes with as much accuracy and detail as possible can be a huge help later. Some of these ideas may mean absolutely nothing and some of them may be some of the most important things you come up with to create success and opportunity in your life.

The sheer fact you are now in a place in your life where you are cataloging your thoughts puts you in a positive successful perspective in life. Cataloging your thoughts causes more thoughts to come to mind, greater ideas are manifested and each of these manifestation can be a great opportunity for success. At the very least your mind is no longer sitting dormant on thoughts which are unsuccessful, unproductive, and useless to your success journey.

When the rush of ideas are pouring in be sure to have a positive mindset and be excited about these ideas. The more emotional excitement you can generate as you are producing these ideas the more excitement and energy is perpetuated. Never approach this idea of cataloging with an "I can't" attitude. Take these ideas and carefully research to see if there are other similar ideas out there on the market. Some of the greatest ideas and inventions are just improvements on something that already exists. Your thoughts and ideas may be a manifestation on the improvement of a product you are already using every day.

Sometimes we take notes or we catalogue ideas and we do research on those ideas and we're stopped dead in our tracks because we feel the idea or the product has already been created. Never ever let an idea go just because you believe it is too closely related to something which is already out on the market. You may show the idea to someone else and another opportunity comes through a collaboration of minds.

The problem with letting an idea go just because you believe it is unoriginal and will find something similar will crush your growth process. It stops your creative energy and then your idea machine sits dormant until you can fire it up again. If you have what you think is an original idea, which after research is too close or already has been invented, just move on to the next idea you have catalogued in your note book.

Even ideas which come to you which seem to be already invented or there is a product already in the marketplace should never be dismissed. These ideas should stay in your idea list or in your idea catalog. The reason you want to keep these ideas on hand is because you may revisit and find later that you can make improvements on the idea. So no idea is a bad idea. No product, no creativity, no inspiration, no poem, no song, no drawing etc. of an idea is a bad idea. Everything which comes from a creative mind is worth keeping, noting and cataloging.

Mind / Time Management

During the process of moving and pushing toward a successful life you should create mind and time management. What this means is that ideas created within your mind which are noted or cataloged should be given an equal amount of time and energy. Stay focus on cataloged ideas in order to generate more positive energy around the idea.

The Secrets of Positive Brainwashing

Take an idea, take an opportunity and put time into it each and every day, week, month until the idea or opportunity has manifested itself into profits. The goal is to make it to the part of the journey in which Trainwashing yourself to note and catalog ideas and thoughts becomes second nature.

So the mind part of the training and re-brainwashing is intact and being utilized but that is where they end their journey. This is the person who spends an enormous amount of energy in the creative stage but they lack balance. So there is no time left for the time management phase.

There must be a balance between mind and time management. The ideas and inspirations which are created by your mind must be cultivated into something profitable. The bottom line is if you do not put enough time and energy into an idea no one else can realize the idea with you. An idea which is not shown to other people or introduced into a market or pushed out on the Internet and shown to others is an idea that isn't any use to anyone.

If you are a type of person for whom your creativity is poem writing or songwriting and you never show one of those poems or song lyrics to anyone else other than yourself it is wasted energy. This does not mean you have wasted your energy on writing the poem or song just that these things are not working for you on your road to financial success. On the other hand if poems or songs are your inspiration and once a week or once a month you introduce one or more of those poems or songs out to the Internet or to friends then you are using great time management for your inspirations. In other words, let the power of people and opportunity work for you.

If you are utilizing good mind and time management then your journey to success and for success will happen much quicker. What happens for the person who shares their ideas, inspirations, and creations is a time multiplication. The more people who see your idea, invention, or product will perpetuate the amount of interest in the idea. It is as if you have many people working for you in a successful company you haven't started yet.

When more people are talking about your idea the results is more energy being spent on this particular idea or creation. This can be a wonderful tool because it means all of the energy you are putting into time management is being multiplied. It's better to have 10, 20, 50, 100 or hundreds of thousand, even tens of thousands of people viewing and talking about a product then having a corner grocery store with only a local presence. There are so many products out on the market today which are complete junk, but they are successful because of the amount of people who are talking about or using the product.

Stop Thinking In The 99 Percentile and Become The Financial 1%

"So be sure when you step, Step with care and great tact. And remember that life's A Great Balancing Act. And will you succeed? Yes! You will, indeed! (98 and ¾ percent guaranteed) Kid, you'll move mountains."

Dr. Seuss

Chapter 5: Vision

Forward Thinking

It is very important you stay in a mindset of forward thinking. Anything less is stagnant. Stagnation means you are not moving forward, which means the journey to success and for success is also not moving forward. If you are in a state of forward thinking your mind is always looking for the next step in the process. The next step in the process could be a huge step or leap forward or it could be a baby step.

The size of the step does not matter. The only thing which matters is the fact you are moving forward or in positive movement, not backward movement or no movement at all. At the end of your note taking, when a new idea hits you, end with "what is the next step? ".

Asking yourself, "what is the next step?" is an open ended statement. The psychology behind this open ended statement is that there is something unfinished in which you need to finish. This should set in your mind you need to go back and work on or complete a task.

An unfinished task should keep the mindset open and keep the creative stream of your mind open. This creative stream should remain open until the question "what is the next step?" is answered. Again this is an open ended statement so even once the question has been answered and written down in your notepad it only leads to asking the question over again. What is the next step?

This is how you train your mind to take baby steps without realizing the process of change in you is happening. Because we all feel lazy or unmotivated at times we need to use little tricks to make ourselves do work when we don't want to do so. If you can create habits which are so subtle you do not feel or recognize they're becoming habits then the feeling of it being a great deal of work is not there. If we can trick the mind into believing the journey is fun, isn't hard work, and doesn't take up a lot of time then we can enjoy the process for a longer period.

Vision Boarding

As we work on changing how our minds deal with note taking, cataloging of ideas, and making these things become habit, we must also stimulate our mind visually for success. We have to realize which visual images are going to motivate us to move toward on our goal for success. Visual stimulation for the mind through "vision boarding" is a wonderful way to help imprint success in the brain.

Vision boarding is taking a board or a space on the wall, a place on your computer, or on your bathroom mirror where you put pictures of things you want to happen in your life. This is where you take bright, colorful, vibrant pictures of the success you would like to achieve and the things you would like to have as you're reaching this pinnacle of success and putting it in front of you each and every day of your life. I cannot stress enough how important vision boarding is in the journey for success.

Overweight people who take images of the body they would like to have when they're trying to lose weight and put the image on a refrigerator or on the mirror where they can see it every day are more likely to succeed in weight loss. People who take a brochure picture of a car they wish to own in the near future and place it in an area where they can see it every day are more likely to receive the car then not.

These are miniature vision boards. The only difference between this and a true vision board is the vision board is a complete map of what you would like to achieve at the pinnacle of your success. This does not mean a vision board does not change over time.

When we first create our vision board and we are cutting out pictures from magazines or printing them to set up our vision board in the beginning does not mean later on we will not change our mind. A vision board should evolve as you become more successful because your wants, priorities, and needs are always changing.

The act of updating and creating new vision boards and new visual stimulation for success only helps to keep the forward momentum going. Changing or creating a new vision board does not mean you are losing focus on the task at hand. In actuality it is the complete opposite. You are creating new fresh focuses which will cause you to motivate yourself forward on the successful journey.

Never remove your visual images or your vision board when you lose motivation. When you lose your forward momentum, or have a hiccup or you take a couple of steps back, the vision board you've created may be the only thing to get you back on track.

See the vision board as a subliminal message as well as a deliberate message. While you're creating the vision board your energy is high and your focus is clear, your motivation is on point, and moving forward. When your mind and your eyes get used to seeing the vision board and it seems you are paying little attention to it subliminally, it's still working for you in a positive manner. So again never remove your visual stimulations from where you can see them each and every day.

Appreciation

There is a certain amount of energy which has to go toward appreciating what you have, where you've been, and where you are going on your journey. In the middle of the journey, the place where we are least likely to remember once we reach our goals and our successes, there have to be high points. There have to be points in the middle of the journey, where we recognize we have overcome an obstacle, where we had to change our path, where we had to rewrite our story in order to become successful.

Everyone has to have a story to tell on their way to becoming successful. How will you tell your story? What will you tell people who are at the beginning of their journey in order to help motivate them? What are the obstacles and situations you'll be able to look back on in the middle of your journey you can truly appreciate? How will you talk about the things you overcame once you are triumphant?

The Secrets of Positive Brainwashing

"Anyone whose goal is 'something higher' must expect someday to suffer vertigo. What is vertigo? Fear of falling? No, Vertigo is something other than fear of falling. It is the voice of the emptiness below us which tempts and lures us; it is the desire to fall, against which, terrified, we defend ourselves."

Milan Kundera, The Unbearable Lightness of Being

Chapter 6: Make Deals

Future Fortune through Early Deal Making

Another important tool I can teach you which you will need to learn in this book is to make business deals though written contracts now rather than later on the success journey. You do not have to be a big businessmen, entrepreneur, or high level salesman in order to make a deal. You do not have to have a bank loan, a million bucks, or friends in high places to make a business deal. You do not have to have a college degree, a business degree, a certificate, or a license of a particular kind to make a business deal.

If you have a skill, an idea, or something to barter, whether it is your own time or an item, practice making business deals. The art of making business deals will help you tremendously on your quest for success. At some point you are going to have to make business deals anyway if you are going to be successful. Therefore the deal-making process should be practice before you become successful.

I recommend to the person who is on their journey and looking for success in life, create five deals per year. This means during a one year period of time there should be at least five deals which are contractually binding in your file cabinet or in a notebook somewhere in your possession.

This does not mean every deal you make has to be with someone else. The reason you should work on five deals per year is because I have found that five deals keeps a good amount of positive pressure on your deal creativity. You may end up doing less than five deals in one year but be sure to focus on accomplishing five complete deals.

We can make creative deals which are binding with ourselves. Here's an example: go online and find a general contractors, specialist or sales contract. You can find these anywhere just by typing contract agreement into an internet search engine.

If you cannot find it or you do not have a printer to print a contract out then go to the library and have them print one out for you. Contract copies will cost between $ .07 cents and $.25 a page (if you cannot do this write a simple contract by hand). Take the contract you had copied and establish a deal with yourself. Don't miss a step.

When you're setting up this deal there should be no shortcuts in how you set up the deal just because it's with yourself. So if you are saying your creative talent is writing poetry set up a contract between you and yourself to create three pieces of poetry each month for the next year.

Whatever you think your niche, specialty, or your gift is, set up a contract agreement which has time constraints, deliverables, quality assurance etc. in a binding contract. Most banks will notarize contract agreements free of charge and you should go this far when setting up the contract agreements.

Go into your local bank to sit down with the notary and have them notarize the contract as a binding agreement. The notary does not have to know the agreement is between just you and no other person. This is how you set up an easy contract and learn what it is to negotiate contract terms in a simple manner as a beginner.

After you have completed setting up a contract between you and yourself then go out and set up a contract with someone else. The contract you set up with someone else can be with a close family member or close friend and maybe there is no monetary benefit to you. There should be little importance on how much money will be made while setting up this next contract with the other person.

Here is an example: set up a contract with the family member where you give them something or do work for them free of charge for a particular duration. Set up a contract with your mother, father, grandmother, an aunt or uncle to rake their leaves, clean out their refrigerator or help them in planting an organic garden. Anything. But make it a binding contract. The contract between a family member and non-family members should be a binding contract signed and notarized by the proper authority.

There should be stipulations, time constraints, deliverables, final contract date, satisfaction guarantee clauses etc. You do not need to understand completely all of the legalities of setting up a contract like this with a close family member. This contract is just to give you practice in negotiating contracts which are preferably win-win for both parties.

"What do I get out of a contract with a family member who does not pay me?" The fact you are helping someone live a better life should be satisfaction enough for setting up this type of contract. Moreover the experience of setting up, negotiating, and completing a contractual deal will be more educational than you can imagine. So that takes care of a couple of your contracts for the year.

Here is another example of an easy contract. Barter your time or something you own against something someone else owns or needs done through a contract. Preferably this person is not a family member. Here you want the experience of negotiating contracts with people you are not extremely familiar with. Check the newspaper want ads, search on the Internet, find something someone needs done which you can barter through a contractual agreement and give them a call.

Don't stop trying to create these contracts until you have at least five contracts on the books. If it takes longer than a year to create these five contracts then this is absolutely fine. Each one of these contracts will give you a boost in how to deal with the middle of the journey to become successful. Each of these contracts will show you and help you to understand how to get over rejections which are going to happen through the journey. Each of these contracts will show you that you can and will persevere in times where there seems to be no way or nothing good happening in your life.

There are other contracts which can be set up and with each contract there should be a higher level of difficulty associated with how the deal is structured. Therefore each contract you create with another person or group should have a greater level of work that has to be put into the agreement.

By the time you get to the fifth contract you're setting up there should be cash, weekly or monthly payments, barter, checks or some sort of monetary exchange.

There are always steps to every process therefore by the time the fifth contract is done you should be a pro at setting up small deals. Some of you will have a learning curve and want to move to more advance deals sooner than later. This is fine as long as the deal structuring and the idea of creating win-win contracts stay the same.

If the mind is set on greed or only what you can gain and not the other party getting a fair deal as well, the deal will not likely manifest or will be broken early. Think about ethics and honor when creating your deals. This is why each deal should be just a little more advanced than the one previous. No monetary exchange until a proper mindset for deal making has been reached.

Stop Thinking In The 99 Percentile and Become The Financial 1%

"All you need in this life is ignorance and confidence; then success is sure."   Mark Twain

Chapter 7: Learn Something New

Building New Mind Bridges

The process of learning something new helps to stimulate creative growth or creative inspiration. It is very important not to fall into a mindset of being stale or losing your creative inspirations. Moreover, learning new tasks is proven to stimulate different parts of your brain. For instance, learning an instrument such as the piano or guitar helps to stimulate neural connection growth in the brain which allows for greater creativity in other areas of your life.

This means indirectly if you were to sit down understand and learn to play the piano you would be creating new ways to put together creative win-win business deals. Anything you can do to spawn creative thoughts will increase your success potential. You are probably thinking up to this point there is a lot of work that has to be done in order to become successful. Yes there is some work to do but everything in this book should be thought of as fun, joyful, and creative, not work.

As you are expressing yourself through new creative ways such as learning an instrument, creating something with your hands, writing a piece of poetry or lyrics to a song you are allowing yourself freedom of thought. It is a good idea to document the feelings that come along with this creative mind bridge building process.

Documenting this new avenue of creativity in which you have tapped into allows you to commit this new behavior into long-term habitual growth. These forms of creativity keep the mind from settling into wasteful nonproductive negative brainwashing habits. So again, anything which takes you away from sitting down and spending most of your hours watching primetime television will move you closer to your goal of success in life.

It is important through this creativity or instituting this creative mindset to make sure you are in a state of creation. Therefore if there is a location which makes you feel comfortable, relaxed emotionally, and without stress make this place the location you go to when you are creating new ideas.

This is the location where you should spend most of your time during the creativity process. There should be good feelings associated with the creative process. If there is a certain type of clothing or a favorite pen or pencil which brings joy to your creative outlet then this item is what you should use as a creative tool. Your creative tools can be anything as long as it is safe, makes you happen, and does not bring harm to others.

There are things you can do to create certain mindsets for performing positive and successful behavior. Try this for example: every time you try to create a contractual agreement put on a suit and dab of cologne or perfume. Put on your favorite jewelry which reminds you of success and only then sit down and create this contractual agreement with yourself or with someone else. This sets the mood for professionalism and seriousness of creating the contractual agreement. It also sets a realization in your mind which is more important than if you were trying to make agreements in a pair of sweatpants and a sweatshirt.

Not everyone has a new suit or a nice dress just hanging in their closet. So if you are a person who does not have the immediate means to change the way you look then go to a thrift store or borrow a suit from a relative. Make sure you look clean and shaven, and ready for success. Do whatever it takes to put yourself in a mindset which will allow you to be creative and put together deals which will train you to be more successful.

The key is to keep your mind out of the state of being poor, financially poor or mentally poor. You want to keep your mindset in the state of riches, success, and always moving forward. You have to feed your mind success and allow your mind to consume success. If you block success in any way you are prolonging the journey to success. Feed your mind only good things and your mind will in turn reward you with good things. If you feed your mind a bunch of crap then you will only get back a bunch of crap.

The Secrets of Positive Brainwashing

"The way to get started is to quit talking and begin doing."

Walt Disney

Chapter 8: Not Enough

It is not enough to free Your Mind

It is not enough to free the mind from its enslaved and imprisoned way of thinking. It is not enough to take the first step to realizing your mind is enslaved and imprisoned to fail. Although realizing these things are all well and good it is just not enough.

Once you realize this within yourself, the fear of success and greatness will loom much larger for a period of time. Just having the realization that these fears are within you causes them to move to the forefront of your thoughts. As these ideas and fears move to the forefront of your mind for a period of time they become difficult to control. Let them go.

The fears one realizes during the middle of their journey to success cannot and should not be debilitating. Once these fears have been recognized they must be realized as something that really doesn't exist. The bottom line is: fear does not exist. We create our own fear and then we let those fears control us.

Here's where the problem comes in because we have thought about fear all of our lives and as a demonstrable part of our life they will be too difficult to let go. It is not enough to say you are going to control your fears, you must control them.

In order to control your fears on the journey to success you must train and retrain them out of the forefront of thinking. Your mind must be "Trainwashed" from the fear state into a state of mind in which fear just does not matter or exist.

Ethos

Find and change your own ethos. Your ethos is your nature or philosophy in which you live at any given moment. Everyone has it within them to change their ethos when it comes to fear and their placement in life at this very moment. You are who you right at this moment but you can choose to be something and someone else. You can choose to be someone deeper, stronger, and more positive right in this very moment.

Your ethos will change over time automatically but you also have the opportunity and ability to change your ethos right now. The characters and fundamentals of life are not set in stone. They can be changed if you become a willing participant in this change. You cannot become a willing participant to change if fear stays in control of your life. Trainwash a new ethos within you and the results will be astonishing.

Maturity of Mind

I believe we all must work towards a "maturity of mind" when it comes to success. What this means to me is that during certain points in your life or in your journey your mind is neither strong enough nor ready to achieve success. There is a lack of maturity to understand how you are to achieve true success on your journey. This does not mean you will not achieve smaller successes during your life, of course you will. But to achieve the ultimate true success your mind must be ready, it must be mature.

If your mind is not mature then you will be unable to handle the wealth that comes with true success. Therefore true success may be short-lived for the person without mind-maturity. Millions upon millions of people around the US and the world play the lottery and some of them even win. Statistically speaking most people who win the lottery is unprepared and they are not mature enough to manage their winnings and new found wealth.

Something which usually happens to people who have gained wealth and fortune" overnight" is that their mind is unprepared to deal with the shock and the change of being able to purchase anything their heart desires. So these people go out and buy things and spend their money. They'll help family and friends financially but never having an actual grasp of how they're managing their wealth.

These people usually do not think about taxes, interest rates, and other financial fees that are associated with great fortune. These people usually become broke and in debt very quickly because of not having mind-maturity. When you are ready for true success you will have clarity of thought and how to manage this success.

The wonderful thing about having mind-maturity is that the actual age of the person does not matter in its achievement. You may be on a journey in which you develop mind-maturity in your 20s while others on the same life journey may take a bit longer to develop mind-maturity. Another wonderful thing about mind-maturity is the fact you can speed up the process at any point in your life.

Therefore a person can be in their 20s and develop their mind-maturity in order to achieve true success and financial wealth. People in the latter part of their life, maybe 50s or 60s, who have not developed mind-maturity, can still achieve this at this point in their life. My suggestion is to develop your mind-maturity early in life so you may enjoy the fruits of your labor for a longer period of time.

Are you ready for mind-maturity and the success that comes with having mind-maturity? If you are not ready for mind-maturity and you are on the journey for true wealth and success then surround yourself with people who are already mind-mature. Find someone who is mind mature and have them mentor you. Having a mentor is a great way to help you develop mind-maturity.

Developing mind-maturity is like opening up your mind's eye or a window of your mind. With this maturity you will be able to see and understand successes on your journey which otherwise would be unrecognizable. You will be able to recognize the potential of what your mind is capable of doing.

When the mind is mature you are almost able to see things before they even happen. It is much like having a crystal ball or a sixth sense which allows you to look into the future, and into your future. So be successful by developing your mind-maturity to its greatest potential.

The Secrets of Positive Brainwashing

"Money was never a big motivation for me, except as a way to keep score. The real excitement is playing the game".

Donald Trump

Chapter 9: Brain Food

<u>Eating For Success</u>

Can food or diet hinder or assist in your ability to be successful in life? It is my belief that food and other consumptions have a direct affect on how successful you can be in life. We know and understand sugar, carbohydrates, salt, soft drinks, alcohol, and other items we consume can have adverse affects on our bodies. It may not affect everyone in the same manner or in the same timeframe, negatively or positively, but what we consume affects everyone. We know bad foods or nutrition affects the human body adversely as well as healthfully.

Therefore wouldn't it be plausible that if your diet is inundated with "unhealthy" food you are likely not to have the proper brain function that is needed in order to be successful. This does not mean if you eat fast food every day you cannot be successful. On the other hand we know eating fast food and packaged foods can lead to slower metabolism.

Slower metabolism can lead to inactivity, lethargic behavior, and lack of energy. So let's think about this for a second. If all of these things lead to the bottom line of lack of energy and lack of energy leads to lack of motivation, then food is directly related to your success. We need high energy levels to move our minds and bodies to a positive place of successful thinking and behavior. If consuming the right foods can possibly assist in reaching a higher level of success more quickly then why not add it to your Trainwashing.

Your body is a highly tuned machine by default. Think about the car you will be driving once you reach the levels of success you seek. Really envision this car by closing your eyes and allowing the picture into your mind's eye. As you are driving this car around you're getting close to running out of gas. How much sense does it make to instead of stopping at a gas station and putting high-octane fuel into the tank to instead pour water or dirt into the gas tank?

Of course without even thinking about it you can understand it would be completely ridiculous to put water or dirt into the fuel cell of any automobile. Yet our bodies, which are worth millions of times more than the most fabulous automobile, we can envision the majority of time putting garbage into the gas tank. There is no way the car you envision can run with water or dirt in the gas tank and there is no way you can run at your highest potential with garbage in your gas tank.

Why leave anything to chance? If you leave anything to chance then there is a chance you will lose on your journey to be successful. So why not take a different approach. Take a baby step and trade out one of your unhealthy meals or snacks for something which is going to give you a bit more energy to be successful on your journey.

Eat to be brain strong, eat to promote healthy living, and eat to promote higher energy levels. People who have higher energy levels tend use the energy to increase the amount of success and the amount of time they spend on building success. If all you can do is come home from work, sit on the couch, eat a box or bag of fast food, and watch television, then you will not find success in that realm. You must do the things which keep you out of the realm where you are forced into a routine that keeps you unsuccessful.

Knowledge is power for everyone so learn more about what you are putting into your body. Read labels to see if there are chemicals in your choices of toothpaste, drinks, food, and hair products etc. There is fluoridation of our water systems. We know there is fluoride in toothpaste and fluoride has been linked to adverse affect on the brain.

We also know there are soft drinks on the market with artificial sweeteners and other additives which are harmful. At the very least these thing are not good for the human body. Are you taking medicines which are aiding in the demise of your brain power? Help yourself to develop and keep your brain running at its maximum potential so there is nothing to slow your journey to success, not even what you consume.

Stop Thinking In The 99 Percentile and Become The Financial 1%

"Remember, do your best to help one person, who will help 10, who will help 100, who will help 1000 others, who will in turn change a million minds with your first action"

Michaelson Williams

Chapter 10: Reaction, Action, Attraction

Responding To Your New Successes

Reaction

Like anything else there will be reactions to the changes which will be taking place in the mind during the "Trainwashing" process. There will be a definite reaction both positively and negatively to the changes which will be happening through this journey to success. How you react to these changes will determine what your level of success is and how long it is going to take to get there.

It is very simple to fall back into old habits when you are trying to Trainwash your mind. Without proper recognition the tendency is to sit dormant and not do anything. This usually happens because of fear. The reactions to the small successes you make as well as the small failures can sometimes end in the same result. In either case there may be a time where you sit dormant or you freeze because you are not used to the success or overwhelmed by the failure. Never fear, these time period can be minimized.

In these times of latent behavior, when fear causes you to freeze and lose motivation, it is important to reset. In essence you are taking a breather. You are gathering yourself. You are building your confidence again and once again you set out on the journey with a positive attitude. There is always going to be negativity on your journey to success. Your will to succeed will always be tested.

There is some odd universal phenomenon which happens when a person makes a decision to change their life in a positive manner. It seems once a person makes up their mind to seriously change their position in life the universe says "I must test your conviction". When the universe changes to see what level of conviction a person has in changing their life to be more successful this is when most people decide to give up. Never give up on the desire to make a better life for yourself and your family. When your convictions are tested you must have a positive reaction to the test.

When your conviction is tested you must not react negatively or freeze up. If you do find you have frozen and become stagnant because of a hiccup in your journey to move forward in success, apply the baby steps. If you do not follow the steps in the process of taking baby steps then it is likely you will stay in this frozen dormant state for too long and then your dreams and goals will dissipate.

When most of us were children we believed we could do anything, even fly and in our minds we were able to do it by envisioning the possibility. What happened? Now some of us do realize something has changed us and we do not have to stay in our negative brainwashed state anymore. We can change and retrain out the negative brainwashing to a positive new brainwashing which supports positive thinking and actions. In other words we can fly once again.

Some of the time when we have troubles during our journey to success we freeze, stopping our forward momentum. Then we let ourselves create excuses. This is the wrong reaction to this phase of the journey. The correct reaction is to recognize the issues and then focus on taking one step forward. Do not focus on taking a quantum leap forward. If you focus on taking a quantum leap forward and start focusing on something which is too far down the road you will cause yourself to go into a repeat phase.

Think about it the same way you would think about having a scratch on a record or CD you want to play music from. If there is a scratch on the CD and the laser does not pick up the next series on the CD, much like a record skipping on the record player that CD will skip and the laser will continue to search for that one bit of information needed to continue playing.

If the laser cannot pick up the next bit of information it tries to move down the road until it can get clean data to finish playing the song or the track in which it was searching. So basically what you want to do is look for the next neighboring track, the next bit of data that is going to allow you to smooth out the trouble spots you are experiencing.

During the time in which you may experience setbacks you have to retrain your processes. Retrain the process which got you to the point you are currently. All the processes you have retrained in your mind Trainwash them again. Remember negative brainwashing does not happen overnight. Therefore positive re-brainwashing or "Trainwashing" (retraining positive brainwashing) will not happen overnight as well.

Because people are not created equal, in my opinion the journey from one person to the next and how they deal with these stopgaps will happen at different time frames. Some people take longer to get over the hiccups, some people do not get over the difficulties, and others can push through with little issue at all.

Try to develop a psychology within yourself which allows you to push through the setbacks in your journey to success. Successful people have to go through the same processes to become successful as people who are unsuccessful at the moment. The difference between the two is how a person who is not negatively brainwashed and a person who is negatively brainwashed deals with the journey to success.

Coaching / Coasting

There are people on their journey to a successful life who need an enormous amount of coaching. On the other hand, there are others who are able to coast. Recognize in yourself as quickly as possible whether you are a "coaching" person or a "coasting" person. If you recognize you are a coaching person then you will understand you need more tools which will allow you to Trainwash your mind for success. Now recognizing you are a coaching person does not mean your journey is going to be any easier or any more difficult, shorter, or longer than a person who is a coasting type of person.

If you are a coasting type of person it does not mean you are going to have a shorter road to success than a coaching type of person. It also does not mean there are different levels of negative brainwashing that has taken place in these two types of people. The only thing it lets us understand is the coasting person needs less visual and mental tools on their journey to achieving a successful life.

Let's not forget in most cases success happens in the mind before it happens in reality. Therefore whether you are a coaching or a coasting type of mindset you still have to visualize your success first. Moreover, the visualization of this success must be sustained; it cannot be a fleeting thought. The reason the visualization of success cannot be a fleeting thought is because there is no positive retraining of the mind from a fleeting thought. Positive "Trainwashing" and retraining of the mind has to be sustained for it to mean anything to the journey or to the visualization of success.

Action

Stop working on" Faith" or at least have faith in yourself first. Instead of faith, choose action on your journey. The reason I say do not use faith in your journey is because faith in a higher (whatever) leads to inaction. Having faith or believing in faith allows you to not do anything which requires true personal action. When you leave it up to faith you are in essence telling your brain and your mind someone else is going to take care of this for me.

The only thing this type of faith belief does is open up enormous gaps in which you are wasting time and energy not moving toward your success and dreams. Remember; do not leave anything to chance. Do not rely on faith to do something you should be doing yourself. The only faith you should have is faith in yourself. Have faith in your actions, not the actions of something you cannot see, hear, or touch.

Now if you are the person who is reading this and saying to yourself all I have is "faith", "I can't do anything without faith". One, you are setting yourself up for failure. Two, your failure is going to come a lot sooner because your forward energy is stopped. If you must believe in faith do not allow your forward momentum and your forward energy to sit dormant waiting for someone to do what you should be doing yourself.

Take action and take responsibility for your own journey. When you get to the end of your journey, and you have achieved true success, whether it is in the mind or in the things you have achieved, you can take credit for the hard work you have done. Take action and keep yourself in action or in a forward moving state of mind and person physically. The longer you can stay in this state of action the further along on the journey to success you will move without realizing it.

Being in the state of action is almost like flying an airplane on autopilot. There will be times when you are moving from point A to point B you feel like you are doing no work at all but things will be happening. When the pilot of an airplane flips the autopilot switch it does not mean his job is done or his presence is no longer required. The pilot still has to monitor the controls but the pilot just does not have to work as hard through all of the navigations. This is what being in a state of action does to the journey of success.

Take action on every opportunity that comes your way. Try to be sensitive to these opportunities and at the very least jot the information down in a notebook so you can return to it later. You want to be able to review the notes from your journey and the opportunities which come during your journey from an analytical standpoint. Later, when you are in the action phase you will have plenty of information to revisit.

You want to be able to review the notes you take down after a vivid dream or something you heard on the radio which caught your attention or an idea of creation you had and be able to analyze the information later on. This is when the action phase is truly important.

Attraction

You want to be able to attract good things in your life. The things you attract should be positive not negative. You want to be able to keep yourself in a positive state of mind and a healthy state of body. A healthy mind and a healthy body will be able to release energy which will attract healthy circumstances.

There are gates, openings in the chakra, or energy of the body which are able to send and receive energy. This is from a philosophical standpoint of life. If these gates are open, other people, successful people, will be able to recognize this in you.

The reason successful people will be able to recognize your gates are open or your energy is high is because they recognize it in themselves. It almost never happens that a person who has low self-esteem, who has a poor self image, who is living in a depressive, depressed world finds themselves making business deals with a multi-millionaire.

The reason this type of scenario does not happen is because there are two different energies from these two types of people. There is an energy which allows success and there is an energy which does not allow for success. The energy which is allowing for success is looking for or able to recognize other energies of the same quality.

Continue keeping your mind, body and energy flowing in a positive successful state of being. Keep in a state of readiness to receive positive successful energy from people who are positive and successful. Smile when you don't feel like smiling. Laugh when you don't feel like laughing. Live when you don't feel like living until successful energy from successful people is able to latch on to the positive energy you create.

If you are down in the dumps, motivate yourself to get out and to interact in a place that brings your energy level up. If you do this I promise you the residuals from being in this type of situation will carry on for a few hours, a few days, even a few weeks or months. The longer you can stay in this high-energy movement and your aura, chakra or energy gates are open the better chance you have of receiving high-energy from others.

"Sometimes life knocks you on your ass... get up, get up, get up!!! Happiness is not the absence of problems; it's the ability to deal with them."

Steve Maraboi, Life, the Truth, and Being Free

Chapter 11: Attitude

Having and Keeping the Proper Attitude

It is incredibly important to have and keep a proper attitude when on the road for success. There is no doubt during your journey your attitude and moods will change. Sometimes things just happen which are no faults of your own that are negative. There may be times when you just get outright bored of trying to keep your energy levels and the excitement of being on the journey at a high level. It just happens and it's okay.

What is not okay is if you treat boredom like it is the end of the world. The biggest and worst things that can happen in the middle of your journey to success will mean little to nothing once you become successful. The only time setbacks matter during the journey is in the moment and at the moment. Once the setback is corrected and the proper positive attitude is applied, the particular setback means nothing. Everything in life is a learning process and setbacks are a part of the learning experiences needed to become a true success.

The problem most people have with dealing with setbacks is they cannot change their attitude. We have a tendency to hold on and dwell on setbacks which happened during our journey to success. Because we spend time and energy focusing on a particular setback we release our negative attitude or emotion and it becomes this gigantic monster. Sometimes we do not even stop there and continue the downward emotional spiral.

There are times we realize we have created a monster and then we want to feed the monster. What we have to remember is the monster only feeds on negativity on a bad attitude and if we change this negativity to positivity and a good attitude the monster cannot feed. Therefore the setback (monster) has to go away and will go away every time. If we can learn to control this quickly we can then correctly and quickly move forward in our journey once again.

An easy way to keep a good attitude during the journey to success is to find things that are fun to do in life. Find something or do something you have never done before. Don't just do things you've experienced before that you find to be fun.

Discover new activities so the experience is brand-new. This will increase the level of joy because it's something your brain views as unfamiliar. Completely new experiences are something your emotion and feelings are not familiar with but they still experience higher levels of happiness during new experiences.

Trying to experience new activities in which you are unfamiliar with also sets a precedent which will take away the fear of trying new things and experiences that will allow you to be successful. Sometimes we do not strive for success because of fear of actually living the experience and having the emotion of which we are unfamiliar. We can imagine what a new experience is going to be like right now. But living the experience in the here and now is almost always much more than we could have ever imagined.

While we are trying to look for and live these new experiences and trying new activities which we have never imagined we must remember these things should be geared toward success. So this doesn't mean if you go out to experience a nightclub and it gives you happiness you continue to relive the experience every weekend. For obvious reasons you do not want to get stuck in a rut of visiting the same place over and over again, trying to relive the initial experience.

For less obvious reasons it slows down the success process. In a situation such as going out to a nightclub and then repeating the experience we allow ourselves to become trapped in the occurrence. Once you are trapped in a particular experience the situations become powerful enough to stop your forward momentum. This is because too much time and focus will be placed on trying to get the same emotional feeling of the first time you experienced this particular situation.

When you are trying to relive the initial new experience it becomes time wasting. Be sure to take yourself out of these types of situations, reset and continue the journey. Find something new you can do once or twice, enjoy it, and then move on. You want to be able to balance playtime and worktime while on the success journey. Your journey to success cannot be all work because if it is you will not want to do it for long.

The journey to success cannot be all play because if it is then you won't be spending the time doing the work making the connections which are going to make you successful. The key is to find the balance in both work and play. The other key is to mix the two by combining work and play.

Keep yourself within arm's length of successful people so you can rub elbows with them on a regular basis. Some of the best and most successful deals you make will be in a social setting not work setting. Try this out, ask someone successful you know or just met if they have ever made a business deal in a non-work environment. I guarantee you almost 100% of the time they will say yes they have or at the very least made an important connection.

One thing I want to mention is while you are "rubbing elbows" with successful people in social situations, be respectful. Do not be the guy or girl that successful people are looking to avoid because all you can talk about is the next deal you are trying to make. If people are putting up walls every time you come around because you can't shut up about some new business deal, something new you have created, or something you want to sell, then your journey to success is going to be slowed down considerably.

Remember to stay balanced in your journey because it may take just a miniscule connection with someone to create a deal or opportunity. In social situations sometimes just a handshake or a passing hello can lead to making the right connections for a future project.

If in a social situation your mind is always on the deal then you are working. Therefore you cannot give off the proper vibe or energy to make a positive connection. On the other hand, if you are having fun during a social event you are giving off the proper vibe or energy to make a positive connection with successful people.

Make sure you have patience. Have patience with the new opportunities. Have patience on the doors opening. Have patience with the people you interact with and most of all have patience with yourself. Things which feel like they are happening overnight or quick money or quick success are usually fleeting or short-lived. You want to strive for long-term success so you only have to take the journey once.

I'm sure you've heard of people who live the rags to riches to rags again stories or the riches to rags and then to riches. I've had friends that were multimillionaires who during the economic crunch lost everything. This proved to be completely devastating to most of them. Not many people can turn their life back around after an overwhelming financial event such as total income loss, even though the journey back to riches is usually not as difficult as the first achievement.

The second time around it is still a journey no one wants to do twice. So keep your mindset not in the quick money but instead the longevity money. Keep your mind in a place where you are thinking of long-term success and the building of long-term connections so you will not be another rags to riches to rags story yourself.

The Secrets of Positive Brainwashing

"In order to be successful in life you must re-train your brain to be a success within. Every person has all the time in the world to accomplish this, but the only world that matters is the one you create for yourself"

Michaelson Williams

Chapter 12: Success Position

The One Percentile and Then There's You

In our country and in our society, as in most, there are different classes of people. We have the mega or super rich, the rich, and the well-off which are still considered part of the upper class. Then we have the middle-class, a lower-class beneath them, and then we have the poor. As time goes on these classifications are moving further apart and larger gaps of financial wealth and well-being are being seen in this country.

Now it seems there is a mega or super rich group who primarily control the world's financial markets and economies. Next in line are the rich who control second-tier business. Then there is or soon will be the people who are barely hanging on. There are people who think they are hanging on and the people who have realized they have already lost. Even though a person can look at their financial statements and deduce where they stand in these groups it is the mind which will determine where your true place of financial wealth lies.

If we were to build a matrix of this financial and economical" who's who" we would say that people who are in the one percentile are at the top of this matrix. Then we complain because we consider ourselves in the 99th percentile who are the" have-nots". The trouble with complaining about this upper echelon of mega rich is that your mind is in the wrong focus.

If you are one of the people who are spending enormous amounts of time worrying about the financial 1% then you are wasting precious time which can be focused on becoming one of them. You are wasting an enormous amount of energy on negativity focusing on why you do not have what this 1% population does.

Guess what? The one percentile is not thinking about what you don't have. The one percentile is focused on what they do have and how they are going to keep it. They are not concerned with you because you have created a world in which you are a non-factor by your actions and attitude.

People who are too focused on what the upper echelon are doing in a negative manner do not have time to raise themselves up to a higher level of financial independence. When you find yourself complaining about what you don't have and what "they" do have in a negative way you are prolonging your journey to success. Change your way of thinking so you can appreciate what the "mega rich" has so that some of their wealth and riches will become some of your wealth and riches.

Most of us know and understand if we wish bad things on other people the universe looks at us, karma comes around, and all of a sudden bad things are happening to you. Therefore why would you wish bad things on people who are more fortunate than you are?

Focus on appreciating what they have so the universe can look at you and see this appreciation and send positive karma to you so you are able to receive wealth. The only difference between the mega rich in the financial one percentile and you is the way you think and the way they think.

Now I am sure there are quite a few people in this upper echelon who look at people who have less with eyes of disapproval or a feeling they are better than this "lower class". I am sure there are some who look at people with less and say and feel lower class citizens do not deserve the great abundance in which the one percentile has achieved. But this is far from the truth. You must understand that you deserve the same financial freedom and happiness as the next person.

I'll have to add a caveat to this statement because if you cannot feel that you deserve this financial freedom, and you refuse to do the work which will change your mind so you can think and feel like the mega rich, then you do not deserve to be there yourself. If you refuse to "Trainwash" or re-brainwash yourself for success then you deserve exactly what you are getting and exactly the situation you are in financially. You are in the exact place in your journey you should be.

What you think of yourself is powerful. Your self-image is the most powerful thing you own because it can determine your level of failure or your level of greatness. Self-image can lift you up and it can also destroy you. The power of your self-image can increase the time or shorten the time in which you are traveling on your journey to success.

Therefore if you are constantly feeding yourself distractions and situations which lower your self-image, things which cause guilt and turmoil, you are not thinking like the successful one percentile. When you start to be able to think better of yourself, you will in turn be able to do better for yourself. You must grasp and hold on to thoughts in which the upper echelon used to be successful and then let them disseminate through the rest of your mind.

Stop Thinking In The 99 Percentile and Become The Financial 1%

"Only those who dare to fail greatly can ever achieve greatly."

Robert F. Kennedy

Chapter 13: Faces

The Look of Entitlement

What is the look of entitlement? If you are not yet thinking and focusing on becoming one of the elite, the upper echelon, the 1%, observe them to see how they carry themselves and their facial expressions. This is not difficult. All we have to do is watch this group, politicians, top business executives, barons, and the mega rich on television. When you observe this group you are going to notice something different about them.

Observe these people very closely. Observe their facial expressions, the way they carry themselves, the way they walk, the way they talk, and you will notice a power about them. You will notice something you do not have at the moment but in which you need to develop during your journey.

You'll notice in the eyes and in the way the elite carry themselves a look of entitlement. The "super" successful create a world within their own minds tells which tell them they are entitled to everything they possess. The look is almost a look of arrogance and there is never any fear in this look.

This look is the expressions which are generated from the depths of the mind which make the super successful believe they are better than you, that they deserve more than you. To put the icing on the cake, this mindset allows the 1% to believe they do not have to work as hard as you and this is what the look of entitlement loans to their ego. Even the people who work like dogs to obtain this mega-rich status at some point will develop the look of entitlement. The look of entitlement is an amazing thing to have because it will open even more doors of opportunity once you have it.

You may be telling yourself well I do not want to have an attitude of arrogance or feeling I am better than someone else. I will tell you this: you and most like you are always ready to serve the people who have the look of entitlement without even thinking about the act of servitude.

The fact of the matter is that almost everyone on this planet believes they are better than someone else. Therefore, if you get into the mindset where you think you do not want to be successful because you do not want to feel like you are better than someone else, you have created an empty excuse for why you shouldn't be successful.

Get rid of the excuse. Take on this powerful demeanor Take on this mindset of entitlement and then if you want to change your way of thinking, do so after you are successful. Do not hold yourself back or slow your journey because you have a feeling of not wanting to be better than anyone else. This is nothing more than a lie you allow yourself to believe in order to stay in the same situation you are in right now. I believe there is nothing wrong with being arrogant as long as it's respectful arrogance. Respectful arrogance is nothing more than confidence in one's self.

I believe holding a sense of entitlement and keeping this mindset lets you know you deserve success and is crucial in your journey. All people have ego. Ego makes you think you are better than someone else at some point in life. There is no way around complete absence of ego in my opinion. Therefore if ego is unavoidable then forget about making excuses which involve the thought of not having ego.

Oxford dictionary defines ego as "a person's sense of self-esteem or self-importance: *a boost to my ego.*" Furthermore, "*Psychoanalysis* the part of the mind that mediates between the conscious and the unconscious and is responsible for reality testing and a sense of personal identity."

You should not allow yourself to make excuses for not being successful because the elite and mega rich are not making any excuses for being successful. If you observe this elite group over a period of time and watch how purchase homes, cars, jewelry etc. you will never see on their faces a look of "I do not deserve this" when they are buying these items.

Instead you only see a look of enjoyment. This look is a natural part of the process. You will see body language as this elite group make purchases which will show you they almost feel as if they do not even have to spend their money to receive these items.

When you have a mindset of entitlement, money is no object. When you possess a mindset of entitlement you are in a state of thinking or being which tells you whether you have money or not, all luxury items already belong to you. I could name numerous mega rich and super successful people I've seen on television making large ticket purchases. When you see them you understand money is the last thing they're thinking about when the receiving these luxuries.

Put yourself in a state of entitlement. "Trainwash" yourself into thinking and understanding even without money the things I want are already mine. Train, retrain and brainwash yourself into thinking everything you want in life you are entitled to receive.

If you want to dig a little bit deeper into your own psyche during the positive brainwashing phase, tell yourself when you meet and interact with people who are more successful than you that are entitled to what they have.

Therefore if you are making a business deal or you are at a social event where there are successful people and you are able to meet them, shake their hands, and in the back of your mind (think), "I am entitled to what you have". If you are able to meet your favorite celebrity and you get close enough to embrace them, have a photo opportunity when get to shake their hand. Tell yourself, I am entitled to what you have.

Now in a way this may feel like stealing but it isn't because you should be thinking about this entitlement in a sharing and positive way. Develop a look of entitlement and your whole demeanor will change.

When you embrace entitlement you are not taking from anyone else. You are not breaking into anyone's home and you are not holding anyone up in a robbery. You are only opening your own mind to a state in which successful people hold all the time. You may as well get used to being entitled as quickly as possible because during your journey the more things you acquire through your success the more your mindset will be changed to acquire more (Entitlement).

So do not dawdle. Do not waste time on thoughts of "I don't want to feel better than anyone else". People are not created equal or have not evolved equally therefore it is okay to feel you are better than someone else. You can feel this way as long as the feeling does not lead to a place where you are willing to hurt another human for selfish gains.

Think about this idea for a second. If we were all equal we would all have the exact same amount of everything: brain power, physical attributes, academic strength, positive outlook, weaknesses etc. Instead we are all at different levels in life. No one on the planet is at the exact same point of anything. The wonderful thing is if you can make yourself understand entitlement you will quickly move up the ladder of success.

"Cherish your visions and your dreams as they are the children of your soul, the blueprints of your ultimate achievements."

Napoleon Hill

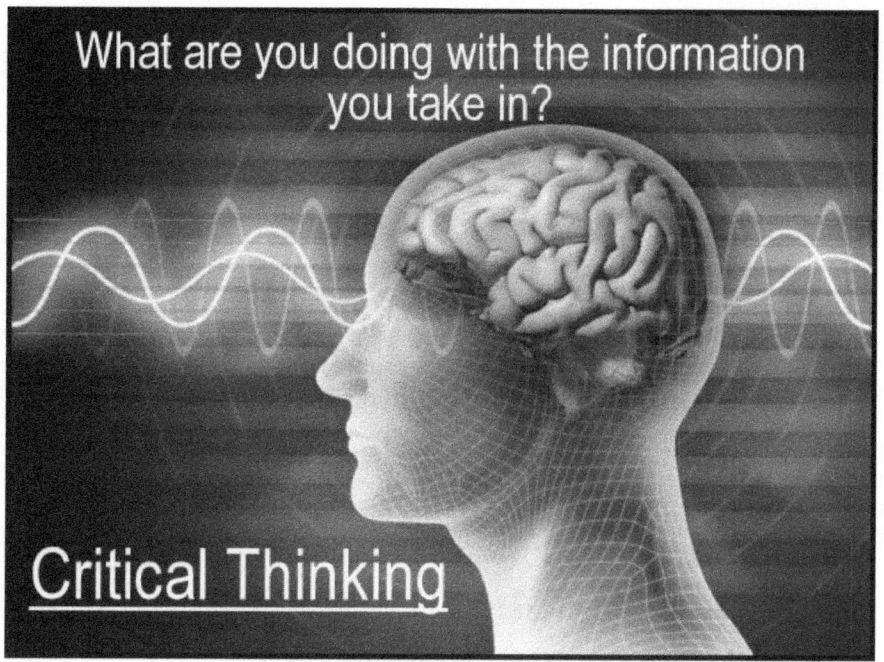

Chapter 14: Thinking / Emotion

Critical Thinking for Success

Critical thinking for success is incredibly crucial on the journey to financial riches. Without critical thinking for success we allow our minds to hold us in a place in which we are unwilling to own up to the reality of our current situation. If you cannot grasp the realization of your current situation through critical thinking and critical awareness, you are destined to stay exactly where you are at this point.

If you do not understand exactly what critical thinking is, look it up, study it, and then train yourself to be a financial critical thinker. Train yourself to be a situational critical thinker. A situational critical thinker allows themselves to look outside of their current state of being and their current state of faults and mistakes in life with an open mind.

This can sometimes be a strange task because for most of us without critical thinking we already feel emotionally the decisions we are making and the steps we are taking are the correct ones to become financially free. In reality what's happening is that by not analyzing and using financial critical thinking and critical thinking, period, we become just another hamster on the wheel of life.

I'm not saying we do not need emotion and feeling to help us become successful. By all means these are great tools and necessary tools to have during the journey to become successful. What we have to do is establish an equilibrium which will allow us to couple our feelings and emotions with situational awareness and financial critical thinking. Another reason we have to use critical awareness and critical thinking during the middle of our journey to success is because it keeps us from making emotional business decisions.

If you allow yourself to make business decisions based on sheer emotions then you are blinded to the fact it may not be a smart decision. Emotional business deals and the use of instincts in business is not the same thing. Financial critical thinking allows us to distinguish between rational and irrational business and financial direction. Irrational business direction is likely driven and fueled by emotion, while rational thinking allows us to pause before we sign on the dotted line.

Critical thinking for success demonstrates we have the ability for financial fair mindedness. Financial fair-mindedness is the ability to make smart critical decisions which lead to success. Learn to find and use the tools of successful people. Learn to think like a successful person. Learn to make decisions in which the upper echelon, the one percentile are making.

Create within yourself an attitude of enough is never enough. This idea of enough is never enough should be based on education first. If you educate yourself with the mindset that enough is never enough, keep a positive attitude, use critical thinking, and live happy, joyful, grateful, and thankful, by default riches will come. Remember, when you are standing on the outside as a person who is a" have not" person looking on the people you consider "the haves" the only difference between them and you is how you think.

You do not need anyone's permission to become successful but your own. No one has to tell you to be successful. You have to start listening to yourself and changing the way you listen to yourself. You have to give yourself permission and say "it's okay for me to be a success in life". This doesn't mean you should listen to your negative self. It means you should give yourself permission to listen to your positive self. Listen to the positive voices in your head which give you small bits of data that are positive instead of negative.

What will you be thinking in the next 30, 60, 90 days, to a year? Will you be the person who is able to Trainwash yourself into success? When you falter will you be able to lift yourself up, rise above the things holding you down, and use critical thinking.

Will you allow your ego to make an enemy of yourself so your journey to success and for success is not delayed? Happiness, wealth and opportunity are at your doorstep and within your grasp all you have to do is retrain your brain to accept the financial happiness in which you deserve.

Congratulations to you for taking these steps, for reading this book, for changing your life. Congratulations to you for realizing it takes more than Faith to become successful. Congratulations to you for realizing it is your own power and energy which is great enough to allow complete success in your life. Congratulations to you for understanding you are entitled to everything you achieve and more.

Stop Thinking In The 99 Percentile and Become The Financial 1%

"Congratulations!
Today is your day.
You're off to Great Places!
You're off and away!"

Dr. Seuss

Chapter 15: The List

The Daily Rules of Trainwashing

Here are the top 20 Trainwashing keys to retrain your brain to reach complete success. This is the road map needed for success here and now, in this day and time.

1. Be open to the belief you are great already.

    You are great already therefore act like it. Your greatness is already within you, you just have to access your own greatness in order to become successful. Many times per day tell yourself that you are great, smart, brain powerful, elite and entitled.
    Do this each and every day to wash the negative brainwashing away.

2. You are what you hold in your mind for the longest time.

    You are what you tell yourself but not just in the moment. It is your sustained thoughts that will make the biggest difference in your Trainwashing. Each and every day hold sustained positive thoughts repeatedly in your head.

3. Help other people become success in some way and it will help you to become successful yourself.

Helping someone else to achieve success will in turn bring greater success to you, if only in attitude. You do not have to help someone build a multimillion dollar business. You can help an old person to cross the street and this will bring you success in that moment.
Do this each and every day to wash the negative brainwashing away.

4. Understand, monitor, and control your own ego as it can shutdown all forward progress on the road to success.
Do this each and every day to wash the negative brainwashing away.

5. Trainwash- Wash the negative brainwashing from your mind and retrain positive ideas, habits, and lifelong positive conditioning instead.
Do this each and every day to wash the negative brainwashing away.

6   Never give up on yourself because you are the most important person on your journey.

You of course are the most important person in your journey to success. Remember this and never try to be successful for someone else. You can use other people for motivation but they cannot be the only reason for your journey. Think to yourself and say "I am the most important person on my journey to success".

7   Smile when you don't feel like smiling. Laugh when you don't feel like laughing. Dance when no one is around, and when there is someone else around dance with them. Be Happy!
Do this each and every day to wash the negative brainwashing away.

8   Fears only exist in your mind, and does not exist without you, so get rid of fear. You create fear.

I want you to really think about this. You create your own fear. Fear does not exist unless you create it. Once you have created fear, however great or small, that fear is only in your mind. Tell yourself each and every day I fear nothing. I am excited for these new opportunities.

Do this each and every day to wash the negative brainwashing away.

9 Be positive, be positive, be positive! You must be positive in your mind so others may see this positivity and want to be in your presence.

Do this each and every day to wash the negative brainwashing away.

10 Create a vision-board. Your vision-board brings the future success into the here and now. Let your vision-board guide you to the things that you want to achieve during your journey.

11 Read books about success and successful people. Read books because true knowledge can only come from a book. Everything else is just sound bites. Information is power; sound bites are distortions in true education and will hurt your journey to success, because you would have not achieved true knowledge. Read a book if only for 5 or 10 minutes a day.

Do this each and every day to wash the negative brainwashing away.

12 Put yourself in positive locations. No matter what, try to find locations that bring you to a positive successful attitude.
Do this each and every day to wash the negative brainwashing away.

13 Work on a healthy body because a healthy body will help you to keep a healthy mind.

This is not just a cliché. If you fuel your body properly your brain will help you produce greater success.
Do this each and every day to wash the negative brainwashing away.

14 Be happy and grateful for what you have right now because there is always someone with less, doing more than you, to achieve success.
Keep in your mind there is always someone with a little less than what you have, a little less social status, financial means, and excuses who is also trying to achieve great success. Let this idea motivate you when

you do not feel motivated on your journey. You aren't the only person who has struggles in life.

15 Forgive others so you are able to forgive yourself, move on, and move forward. Let "it" go, whatever "it" is. Everyone has issues they will not let go in life. If you feel someone has harmed you or done you wrong in some way, let it go. This is poison and will hurt your journey to success.

16 Eat right more than not in order to fuel your brain so that your brain and complete physical conditioning is at its tip top share. Feed your body right as not to poison yourself with chemicals which lead to lowered brain and physical energy and action/activity.
Do this each and every day to wash the negative brainwashing away.

17 Use your time wisely. Success can only come to you if you manage your time properly.

18 Do not stay focused on the small problems that will not mean anything tomorrow. Don't let every small problem that comes up become bigger than what it really is and

then dwell on these issues for hours and days. Tomorrow the problem will be gone and you have wasted too much energy on the problem.

Do this each and every day to wash the negative brainwashing away.

19 Be educated, not smart. Educated people realize just how much they do not know while smart people cannot realize just how unintelligent they truly are.

20 Find a mentor(s). Make sure your mentor is someone who is at a status in life much greater than yours. This means during your journey you are likely and encouraged to find different mentors.

Remember do not waste time on things that will not bring you success. Do not waste time on people who are not interested in true success. Wasted time management and people management will only slow your journey to success.

Trainwashing Learning Tools

Recommended "Trainwashing" Books List: These are books which I found extremely useful while retraining my brain from the negative life-long brainwashing to positive brainwashing for a long life of success wealth and riches. If you do not enjoy reading you can find these titles on the internet as audio books or rent some of them on video or Netflix.

1. Webster's Dictionary- Building your vocabulary
2. Think and Grow Rich by: Napoleon Hill
3. The Magic of Thinking Big by: David J Schwartz Ph.D.
4. The Gerson Therapy by: Charlotte Gerson and Morton Walker D.P.M.
5. The Secret by: Rhonda Byrne
6. The Snowball: Warren Buffett and the Business of Life by: Alice Schroeder
7. Trump Never Give Up: How I Turned My Biggest Challenge into Success by: Donald J. Trump, Meredith McIver
8. Family Wealth: Keeping it in the Family by: James E. Hughes Jr.

9   Excuse Me, Your Life is Waiting: The Astonishing Power of Feeling by: Lynn Grabhorn

10 The Law of Attraction: Esther and Jerry Hicks

TO CONTACT THE AUTHOR, PLEASE WRITE OR EMAIL:

Michaelson Williams

306 Berlin Way

Morrisville, NC 27560

USA

(919) 673-0941

criticalthinking@michaelsonwilliams.com

http://michaelsonwilliams.com

http://imcloudfit.com

HWFnet, LLC.

http://hwfnet.com

(919) 651-8006

1-855-590-8693

OTHER MATERIAL BY MICHAELSON WILLIAMS

http://www.michaelsonwilliams.com

Books

I'm Core Fit: Success in One Day for the Rest of Your Life!

The Adventures of CT: The Children's Books for Adults

Series

Volume 1: The Beginning

Volume 2: Words of Honor

Volume 3: I Will

Volume 4: The Green Machine

Articles

Expert Author

Ezine Articles

http://ezinearticles.com/?expert=Michaelson_Williams

Blog

http://blogoyle.blogspot.com/

Reference:

Ego. 2011. In *Oxford Dictionary Online*
   Retrieved November 3, 2012, from
   http://oxforddictionaries.com/definition/american_english/ego?region=us&q=ego

Quotes retrieved November 3, 2012, from
http://www.imcloudfit.com

Quotes retrieved November 3, 9, 10, 24 2012, from
http://www.goodreads.com/quotes/tag/success

Quote retrieved January 25, 2013 from
http://www.michaelsonwilliams.com

www.ingramcontent.com/pod-product-compliance
Lightning Source LLC
Chambersburg PA
CBHW020744100426
42735CB00037B/479